GREAT BOOK OF
SCHOOL
JOKES

Meridith Berk & Toni Vavrus

Illustrated by Jeff Sinclair

STERLING PUBLISHING CO., INC.
NEW YORK

Library of Congress Cataloging-in-Publication Data

Berk, Meredith.
      Great book of school jokes / Meredith Berk and Toni Vavrus ;
illustrated by Jeff Sinclair
         p.   cm.
      Includes index
      ISBN 0-8069-0782-7
      1. Riddles, Juvenile. 2. Schools—Juvenile humor. [1. Riddles. 2.
Jokes. Schools—Wit and humor.] I. Vavrus, Toni. II. Sharpe, Jim, ill.
III. Title.
PN6371.5.B39 1994
818´.540208—dc20   94–18870
                                                CIP
                                                AC

10 9 8 7 6 5 4 3 2 1

Published by Sterling Publishing Company, Inc.
387 Park Avenue South, New York, N.Y. 10016
© 1994 by Meredith Berk and Toni Vavrus
Illustrations © 1994 by Jeff Sinclair
Distributed in Canada by Sterling Publishing
c/o Canadian Manda Group, One Atlantic Avenue, Suite 105
Toronto, Ontario, Canada M6K 3E7
Distributed in Great Britain and Europe by Cassell PLC
Villiers House, 41/47 Strand, London WC2N 5JE, England
Distributed in Australia by Capricorn Link (Australia) Pty Ltd.
P.O. Box 6651, Baulkham Hills, Business Centre, NSW 2153, Australia

Sterling ISBN 0-8069-0782-7

Contents

1. GETTING TO SCHOOL

Why didn't the young rooster crow in the morning?
It was a little chicken.

How does the abominable snowman clean his teeth?
With an ice pick.

How do you groom a rabbit?
With a hare (hair) brush.

What road do tiny biting insects travel on?
The flea way (freeway).

Why did the little kid go to school on Saturday?
He wanted to be in a class by himself.

Why did the little kid put his clock on the stove?
He wanted to see time fry.

What did one clock say to the other clock?
"Give me a hand."

What part of a clock is never new?
The second-hand.

How would you describe a story about a kid who lost his watch?
Timeless.

Knock-knock.
　Who's there?
Venison.
　Venison who?
Venison rises, it's time
to get up.

Knock-Knock.
　Who's there?
Meyer.
　Meyer who?
Meyer slow getting out
of bed!

Knock-Knock.
　Who's there?
Europe.
　Europe who?
Europe early today.

Knock-Knock.
　Who's there?
Dispatch.
　Dispatch who?
Dispatch on my jeans
is coming off.

Knock-Knock.
　Who's there?
Taiwan.
　Taiwan who?
You Taiwan and I'll tie
the other.

Knock-Knock.
　Who's there?
Cinema.
　Cinema who?
Cinema (Cinnamon)
toast for breakfast.

Knock-Knock.
　Who's there?
Russian.
　Russian who?
Russian to school
makes me tired.

Taking Care of Your Teeth by Pearl E. White

Entering the School by Doris Open

Knock-Knock.
　Who's there?
Manner.
　Manner who?
Manner you late!

　　　Knock-Knock.
　　　　Who's there?
　　　Czar.
　　　　Czar who?
　　　Czar you ready?

　　Knock-Knock.
　　　Who's there?
　　Gobi.
　　　Gobi who?
　　Gobi (go be-) fore it's
　　too late!

2. KINDERGARTEN

Why can't the three bears get in their house?
Goldy locks the door.

Why couldn't Jack become king?
Because he broke his crown.

Why did the kindergarten student want a new pencil?
The one she had made too many mistakes.

Why did Miss Muffet sit on a tuffet?
That's the whey (way) she sat.

What storybook character writes his own songs?
Rap Van Winkle.

Who carries a basket and runs around the forest stealing from the rich?
Little Red Robin Hood.

How did the rabbit beat the tortoise?
By a hare (hair).

What kind of stories do rabbits like best?
Ones with hoppy endings.

EXTRA CREDIT

What did Noah use to build the ark?
Two-by-twos.

TONGUE Twisters

...SAY THESE 3 TIMES QUICKLY!..

Mary's sleepy sheep slept through school.

A new gnu and a blue ewe.

Knock-Knock.
   Who's there?
Ringo.
   Ringo who?
Ringo round the mulberry bush.

"Yes, I would like to sail with Wynken and Blynken," Tom nodded.

3. MATH CLASS

What do you call an arithmetic teacher who can make numbers disappear?
A mathemagician.

How far open were the windows in the math class?
Just a fraction.

If you eat two-thirds of a pie, what do you have left?
An angry mother.

How did the math teacher paint a picture?
By the numbers.

What did the math classroom have instead of desks?

Times tables.

Why did the multiplication table get in trouble with the girls?

He was a two-timer.

What did the math teacher order for dinner?

Cubed steak.

What did the math teacher order for dessert?

Pi.

How does a mathematician plow his fields?

With a protractor.

How do you plow underground fields?

With a subtractor.

What do you call it when geometry teachers use bad language?

Sphering (swearing).

What do geometry teachers have on their floors?

Area rugs.

What did the bee say when it solved the problem?

"Hive got it!"

If a train is travelling in one direction at 50 miles per hour and another train is coming towards it at 25 miles per hour, when will they meet?
Sooner than they want to.

How did the little kids like learning addition?
They thought it was a real plus.

What do you call 144 cockroaches?
Gross.

READING LIST!

Negative Numbers by Morris Les

Basic Math by Adam Upp

Collecting Money by Bill M.

Arithmetic Tests by Kenny Ad

Making the Most of Your Allowance
by E.Z. Munny

Why couldn't the math student get any attention?
He didn't count.

Why was the math student so bad at decimals?
She couldn't get the point.

Which member of royalty is best at math?
The Count.

What would you get if you crossed a dog and a calculator?
A friend you can count on.

What would you get if you crossed an electronic clock with a German shepherd?
A digital watch dog.

What do arithmetic teachers put on after a shower?
Math (bath) robes.

Why couldn't the seven and the ten get married?
They were under eighteen.

How did the student get the answer to ten minus ten?

He zeroed in on it.

Knock-Knock.
  Who's there?
Chesapeake.
  Chesapeake who?
I want Chesapeake at
your money.

Knock-Knock.
  Who's there?
Axis.
  Axis who?
Axis (ask us) again
tomorrow.

...SAY THESE 3 TIMES QUICKLY!..

Double digit decimals.

Three free fast frogs.

Carlton should count chopped chives.

"And then I added it up again,"
Tom recounted.

4. SOCIAL SCIENCES

What do Eskimos put their houses together with?
Iglue.

Who is the coldest relative on earth?
Aunt Arctica.

What's the coldest city in Germany?
Brrr-lin (Berlin).

What would you get if you crossed a river and a desert?
Wet and thirsty.

Where do small dogs like to live?
Lapland.

Are you going to visit Egypt?
I sphinx so.

What's the most precise body of water?
The Specific Ocean.

What do the natives of Peru write with?
Inca.

What's the shakiest National Park?
Jellostone.

Why is it so hard to get into the Everglades?
They're always swamped.

What is the biggest jewel in the world?
The Emerald Isle.

What do Eskimo newlyweds ride on?
An icicle built for two.

What did one person from Holland say to another person from Holland?
"Let's go Dutch."

"I think we're approaching an iceberg,"
Tom said coldly.

What did the explorer say when he found a 5,280-foot rock?
"Now, this is a milestone."

Where can you find lots of shoes?
In the foothills.

Where can you find a character from Alice in Wonderland?
Cape Mad Hatter-as.

What is purple, has a lot of coral and lies in the ocean near Australia?
Grape Barrier Reef.

Knock-Knock.
   Who's there?
Jamaica.
   Jamaica who?
Jamaica my dinner?

Knock-Knock.
   Who's there?
Yukon.
   Yukon who?
Yukon open the door now.

Knock-Knock.
   Who's there?
Kenya.
   Kenya who?
Kenya stop asking
stupid questions and let me in?

Knock-Knock.
   Who's there?
Nome or Chile.
   Nome or Chile who?
It's Nome or Chile today
than it was yesterday.

Knock-Knock.
   Who's there?
Bali Hai.
   Bali Hai who?
Bali Hai up here—
don't look down!

Knock-Knock.
   Who's there?
Juno.
   Juno who?
Juno the way to San Jose?

Knock-Knock.
   Who's there?
Abyss.
   Abyss who?
Abyss (a miss) is
as good as a mile.

EXTRA CREDIT

Why were the African lions so quiet?
They veldt bad.

Several sunny states.

Single Zulus search zealously.

Kings climb cliffs.

5. ENGLISH CLASS

TEACHER: Why is the room buzzing?
STUDENT: We're getting ready for the spelling bee.

TEACHER: Can you spell atrociously?
STUDENT: Sure, and I have the F to prove it.

Can you tell me one word that contains all six vowels?
   Unquestionably.

Why did the a, e, i, o, and u get in trouble?
   For using vowel (foul) language.

22

What do you call two graphs?
A paragraph.

Why didn't the English student want to write poetry?
She heard that rhyme didn't pay.

What happened when the English class started writing poetry?
Things went from bad to verse.

What is the most mathematical part of speech?
The add-verb.

How often do English teachers talk about grammar?
Noun then.

What part of English are prizefighters best at?
Punch-uation.

What did the little kid use to write his essay about the beach?
Sandpaper.

What did the messy student write with?
A pig pen.

What did the little stream have to do for English class?
A brook report.

ALPHABETICALLY YOURS

What letter of the alphabet can fly?
The J.

What are the three least friendly letters?
NME.

What letter is small and green?
P.

What letter does a sailor love?
The C.

What letter is most in debt?
O.

What letters are the smartest?
The Ys.

What two letters are the most jealous?
NV.

What are the two coldest letters?
IC.

ALPHABETICALLY YOURS

What letters have nothing in them?
MT.

What are the two youngest letters?
BB.

What two letters smell terrible?
PU.

What two letters are surrounded by water?
IL.

What are the busiest letters?
NRG.

What two letters grow inside a fish tank?
LG.

What three letters are a musical instrument?
PNO.

What two letters can paint?
RT.

ALPHABETICALLY YOURS

What letters are a flower?
PNE.

What is the most curious letter?
The Y.

What two letters might a Native American
live in?
TP.

What letters are always laughing?
TE.

What letters go with the Beast?
BUT.

... SO, YOU'RE A CHIHUAHUA?

C!

GOTCHA

YOU: Say and spell "M-O-O-D."
FRIEND: Mood—M-O-O-D.
YOU: Say and spell "F-O-O-D."
FRIEND: Food—F-O-O-D.
YOU: Say and spell "B-R-O-O-D."
FRIEND: Brood—B-R-O-O-D.
YOU: Say and spell "H-O-O-D."
FRIEND *(will probably say)*: Hoo-ood.

...SAY THESE 3 TIMES QUICKLY!..

Brenda Brand bought books.

Willy wrote really well.

Please print plainly.

6. TIME TO EAT

YOU'VE GOT A PRETTY BIG **LEEK** HERE MA'AM!

TONY'S PLUMBING

What are a plumber's favorite vegetables?
Leeks.

What do vegetables wear when they get married?
Onion rings.

What is the prettiest vegetable?
Cute-cumber.

What food makes an Alaskan husky run?
Mush.

What is the quietest food?
Corned beef hush (hash).

Why did the silly farmer mow his cabbage patch?
He wanted to raise cole slaw.

Where does a vegetarian lawyer go?
To squash court.

Knock-Knock.
Who's there?
Turnip.
Turnip who?
Turnip (turn up) the heat.

Why do winemakers always know the latest gossip?
They hear it on the grapevine.

What did they have for breakfast on the farm?
Goat-meal.

Why did the silly kid keep staring at the orange juice container?
It said "concentrate."

How do tiny insects cool their lemonade?
With lice cubes.

How do cats cool their lemonade?
With mice cubes.

What do uncles bring to picnics?
Aunts.

What soup talks the most?
Clam chatter (chowder).

How do the gods serve their soup?
With the Big Dipper.

How do they fry their eggs in Never-Never Land?
With a Peter Pan.

What did the two pieces of bread say as they leaped into the oven?
"We're going to be the toast of the town!"

READING LIST!

Making Fruit Salad by Cora D. Apple

Mashed Carrots by B.B. Food

Disgusting Foods by Henrietta Moth

Clamming Up by Shel Fisch

What did the baker say to the bread?
"I knead you."

How did the baker protect his bagel?
He put lox (locks) on it.

How did the sea lion show he liked his lunch?
He gave it the seal of approval.

What did the saucepan and the casserole do when they got angry?
Took pot shots at each other.

Knock-Knock.
  Who's there?
Phillip D.
  Phillip D. who?
Phillip D. soup bowl.
I'm ready to eat.

Knock-Knock.
  Who's there?
Venice.
  Venice who?
Venice dinner?

What kind of sandwiches do sailors eat?
　　Submarines.

Why was dinner late?
　　The cook ran out of thyme.

Why did the teakettle get tired?
　　It ran out of steam.

Knock-Knock.
　　Who's there?
Polynesia.
　　Polynesia who?
Polynesia cracker.

Knock-Knock.
　　Who's there?
Muffin.
　　Muffin who?
Muffin ventured, muffin
gained.

TONGUE Twisters

Sue sold Sam's share of shrimp.

Sherry surely chose cheese well.

Felix fried fish.

Fried fish feel flaky.

Brenda Black brought brownies.

Jumping, jiggling, jerking Jello.

Pluck plump prunes.

Should she chew cheese?

Could Charles—should Charles—chew cheap cashews?

Sam thinks soup stinks.

Edna ate eighty-eight plates of bait.

Betty brought broth she bought.

Few fisherman fry fish.

How did the hot dog wear its hair?
In a bun.

What kind of pizza do dogs like?
Pupperoni.

Why didn't the pie crust get a job?
It was too flaky.

This chicken is so old, it knew Colonel Sanders when he was a private.

"I love spaghetti," Tom said saucily.

"The turkey is very good," Tom was stuffed.

"These potato chips sure are fresh," Tom said crisply.

"I like chocolate candy bars with nuts," Tom snickered.

"I think I swallowed a frog," Tom croaked.

"I don't like fermented grapes," Tom whined.

"I don't like living with pigs," Tom snorted.

What game show do butchers like?
Veal of Fortune.

Why wouldn't the pig make any sounds?
It was dis-grunt-led.

What spot on a Monopoly board do pigs avoid?
Pork Place.

Why did the turkey cross the road?
To get away from the Pilgrims.

What kind of beef do detectives like to eat?
Steak (stake) out.

Why did the butcher's assistant get fired?
He was caught chop-lifting.

Why did the reporter rush into the ice cream shop?
He was looking for a scoop.

Why didn't the seafood salad get along with the rest of the dinner?
It was too crabby.

Why couldn't the dessert reach the table?
It was a shortcake.

What kind of cake should you eat standing on your head?
Upside down cake.

How did the other nuts know the cashew was shy?
He wouldn't come out of his shell.

FAMOUS LAST WORDS

Marshmallow: "Whoops, here comes the chocolate."

Chicken: "Colonel who?"

7. RECESS

What kind of fish is good at Old Maid?
  A card shark.

How often did the teacher read magazines?
  Periodically.

What did the doctor boat say to the father boat?
  "It's a buoy!"

What do you call a cattle tug-of-war?
  Beef jerky.

How are ties tortured?
  They're usually put on the rack.

Why did the girl keep her watch in her piggy bank?
She wanted to save time.

Who sits by himself and puts things in order?
The Lone Arranger.

What playing cards do the most outrageous things?
The crazy eights.

Why did the silly player bring scissors to the card game?
To cut the deck.

How does a fake travel?
By Phony Express.

A kid went out in the middle of a storm with no umbrella. Why didn't she get wet?

It was a sandstorm.

What animal do you need to make a chain?

A lynx.

What's hot and cold,
New and old,
Can't be bought,
And can't be sold?

An idea.

When will my ship come in?

Schooner or later.

8. HISTORY CLASS

Why did the tyrannosaurus wear a Band Aid?
He had a dino-sore.

Knock-knock.
Who's there?
Dinosaur.
Dinosaur who?
Dinosaur you at the mall.

What Dinosaur worked closely with the Lone Ranger?
Tontosaurus.

Why did the student miss history class?
He had the wrong date.

What was Adam's favorite food?
Spare ribs.

Knock-Knock.
  Who's there?
Babylon.
  Babylon who?
Don't Babylon—just open the door.

What historical character was always eating?
Attila the Hun-gry.

Why didn't Socrates like the French fries?
Because they were made in ancient Greece.

Was Rome built in a day?
No, it was built in Italy.

What did they call Caesar when he fell into a vat of dye?
Orange Julius.

Why were the Mongols in such good shape?
They were always going up and down the steppes.

What was the name of the famous Mongolian who conquered nothing?
Genghis Kahn-not.

How did the Vikings tell secrets?
  In Norse code.

What explorer was best at sports?
  Marco Polo.

Where did King Arthur keep his dromedaries?
  In a camel lot (Camelot).

What's another term for the Middle Ages?
  Knight time.

What pirate told the most jokes?
  Captain Kidd.

What would you get if you crossed the Hundred Years War with the War of the Roses?

Very old flowers.

What would you get if a famous French general stepped on a landmine?

Napoleon Blownapart (Bonaparte).

Why did the Pilgrims cross the Atlantic in the *Mayflower*?

It was too far to swim.

Why did the king draw such straight lines?

He was a ruler.

What kind of drink do you get from the Fountain of Youth?

Punch (Ponce) de Leon.

Why did Columbus cross the ocean?

To get to the other tide.

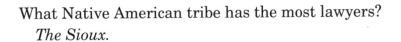

Where did Montezuma go to college?

Az Tech.

What Native American tribe has the most lawyers?

The Sioux.

TEACHER: How many men signed the Declaration of Independence?

JOEY: Our four fathers (forefathers).

Did you know Lincoln's assassin had a table in a diner named after him?

They call it the John Wilkes Booth.

What famous American squashed apples?

Johnny Appleseed.

What was Alexander Graham Bell's brother's name?

Ding Dong Bell.

Why are politicians always in such a hurry?

Because they have to run for office.

Where does the president keep his papers?

In his cabinet.

Knock-Knock.
  Who's there?
Abyssinia.
  Abyssinia who?
Got to go, Abyssinia (I'll be seeing you).

Knock-Knock.
  Who's there?
William Tell.
  William Tell who?
William, Tell your father
to put his bow and arrow down!

Spotting the Enemy by C.M. Cumming

How to Find Things by Luke A. Round

Davy Crockett in Texas by Al A. Moe

Knock-Knock.
  Who's there?
Athena.
  Athena who?
Athena Greek Goddess.

Knock-Knock.
  Who's there?
Warren.
  Warren who?
Warren peace.

45

What did one wheel say to the other wheel?
"Let's go for a spin."

... SAY THESE 3 TIMES QUICKLY!..

Magellan journeyed joyously.

Restless rustlers wrestle cows.

Sir Sully stows thrones.

Columbus' ships sailed surely.

9. MUSIC

Why did the music students get into trouble?
They were passing notes.

Why did the fish make such a good musician?
He knew his scales.

What birds play music at the beach?
Sandpipers.

What do you call it when a violin player runs
away?
Fiddler on the hoof.

What kind of music do old clothes like best?
  Rag-time.

What kind of music did the door knocker like?
  Rap.

What kind of music do insects like?
  Bee-bop.

What kind of music do insects like to dance to?
  Buggy woogie.

Why did the cat turn on the radio?
  She liked mew-sic.

What musical instrument do cats like to play?
  The mew-kulele (ukulele).

Nick needlessly noodled new notes.

Creepy chirping crickets.

Benny broke Drake's banjo.

Trina tried tooting trumpets.

What instruments do trees play?
Woodwinds.

What kind of rug was on the floor of the ballroom?
Waltz to waltz carpeting.

How do you repair an orchestra?
With a Band Aid.

What was the band's favorite lunch?
Tuba fish sandwiches.

How do you tie up a band leader?
With a long chord (cord).

Where did the composer write
music?
In a notebook.

Why did the boy put his records in the trash compactor?

He wanted to make compact discs.

What do you call a short drummer with good rhythm?

A metro-gnome.

Where do musicians buy supplies?

Fife (Five) and dime stores.

What do musicians have on their beds?

Sheet music.

Why couldn't the singer get in the house?

She had the wrong key.

What would you get if you crossed a giant ape and a Chinese musical instrument?

King Gong.

What song did the coffeepot sing?

"Whistle while you perk."

READING LIST!

Good Harmony by B.N. Tune

Knock-Knock.
Who's there?
Tuna fish.
Tuna fish who?
Tuna fish and it'll sing on key.

Knock-Knock.
Who's there?
Tschaikovsky.
Tschaikovsky who?
Gesundheit.

Knock-Knock.
Who's there?
Cello.
Cello who?
Cello, how are you?

Knock-Knock.
Who's there?
Icing.
Icing who?
Icing you a song
if you open the door.

Knock-Knock.
Who's there?
Tenor.
Tenor who?
Tenor eleven times I've
knocked.

10. SCIENCE CLASS

What part of your body has the best sense of humor?

Your funny bone.

What part of your body is the noisiest?

Your ear drum.

What's the noisiest part of your hand?

Your ring finger.

What part of your mouth has the best vision?

Your eye teeth.

What can you hold but never touch?
Your temper.

Why is blood so boring?
It always runs on in the same vein.

How does Dracula get blood from a
meteorologist?
From the weather vein (vane).

How did the meteorologist feel about clouds?
Pretty cirrus (serious).

What did the weatherman get when he stepped
outside into the storm?
A cold front.

Why did the weatherman bring a bar of soap to
work?
He was predicting showers.

What do clouds wear in their hair?
Rainbows.

What does the universe have in common with a
candy store?
A Milky Way.

What is the happiest thing in the sky?
The sun. It's always beaming.

What would you call it if the sun never set from January to December?

A light year.

What happened when the light broke the law?

It went to prism.

What scientific instrument do you use to serve very tiny portions of ice cream?

The micro-scoop.

What was Isaac Newton's brother's name?

Fig.

TEACHER: Why did you fall off your chair?
CLASS CLOWN: I was just demonstrating the law of gravity.

TEACHER: What's a gnu?
CLASS CLOWN: Nothing much. What's a gnu with you?

What do you call a ghost cow?

Moo-sterious.

What petroleum doesn't have any manners?

Crude oil.

What did one skeleton say to the other skeleton?
"I have a bone to pick with you."

What does a skeleton use for skating?
Its shoulder blades.

Why did the boy have a hat on his leg?
It was a knee cap.

Where do you buy used arms for robots?
At a second-hand store.

What game do astronauts like to play?
Moon-poly.

Knock-Knock.
   Who's there?
Spearmint.
   Spearmint who?
Spearmint (experiment) was done in
chemistry.

Knock-Knock.
   Who's there?
Water.
   Water who?
Water you doing?

W...A..T..E...R...

Knock-Knock.
   Who's there?
Amoeba.
   Amoeba who?
Amoeba (I need a) rest.

Knock-Knock.
   Who's there?
Geo.
   Geo who?
"Geo (the old) grey
mare, she ain't what
she used to be..."

COMPUTER Y'S

What do airports and computers have in common?
Terminals.

How did the computer programmer get out of prison?
He used the escape key.

When are computers nice to have around?
When they're compatible.

Why did the school computer get along so well with the failing student?
It was loser (user) friendly.

Old computers never die, they just lose their memories.

Why did the cat hang around the computer?
She was trying to catch the mouse.

EXTRA CREDIT

What microscopic animal solves mysteries?
Perry Mecium.

What would you get if you crossed vegetables with a necklace?
A food chain.

What do you call angry bacteria?
A cross culture.

How much was the science student paid?
A cent-a-grade (centigrade).

Why was the month so worried?
Its days were numbered.

What do you call a blue-white metal?
Zinc about it.

FAMOUS LAST WORDS
Hydrogen atoms: "Let's split."

Knock-Knock.
  Who's there?
Eye whites.
  Eye whites who?
Eye whites you a letter
since you won't let me in.

...SAY THESE 3 TIMES QUICKLY!..

Science shows sea shells shelter sea creatures.

Caves cause close shaves.

Bright blue bats.

Finding Cloud Formations by I.C.A.Duck

Small Computers by P.C. Jr.

Nasty Weather by Gail Force

How to Predict the Weather by Luke Upp

What Is a Vacuum? by M.T. Space

Looking at the Stars by C.D. Skye

How to Use a Telescope by Seymour Starrs

11. GYM CLASS & OTHER SPORTS

Why did the basketball player bring a glass of water to gym class?

So he could learn how to dribble.

Why was the kangaroo invited to join the basketball team?

He was good at jump shots.

What bird is the best weightlifter?

The crane.

What is an athlete's favorite candy?

Tourna-mints.

I'd Rather Watch a Marathon by C.M. Run

Work-Out Clothes by C.R. Shortz

Fighting Fatigue by I.M. Beat

Who's on First? by Ida No

Jack Be Nimble by Jack B. Quick

How to Play Football by N.A. Huddle

Swimming Lessons by Clementine

Toe-Touching Exercises by Ben Dover

What's the best animal to take along when you go swimming?
   The gi-raft (giraffe).

What would you get if you crossed a bowling alley with a knitting school?
   Pins and needles.

Why don't nature lovers like to play badminton?
   They don't want to hit the birdie.

What is the noisiest sport?
   Racquetball.

What's the world's longest punctuation mark?
The fifty-yard dash.

How did Pinocchio win all the races?
By a nose.

Why were all the hurdle events cancelled?
It wasn't a leap year.

Why did the athlete lose the decathlon?
He had a slipped discus.

Why did the wrestler always carry a key?
To get out of hammerlocks.

Why did the dog run out on the baseball field?
It was time for the seventh-inning fetch (stretch).

Why was the spider one of the most valuable members of the ball team?
It was good at catching flies.

What do catchers eat dinner from?
Home plate.

How does a trombone reach second base?
Slide.

Why weren't the boys allowed to play baseball on the farm?
Because they kept hitting fowls (fouls).

What do dogs do before football games?
They hold pup (pep) rallies.

How do professional football players eat chili?
Out of souper bowls.

Who is the handsomest school athlete?
The sprinter, because he's always dashing.

What did the jockey wear on his feet?
Saddle shoes.

What is the worst part of the year for mountain climbing?
The fall.

How can you tell when you've insulted a golf ball?
It gets teed off.

Three free throws.

Wimpy wrestlers wring wet wrists.

Sluggish shortstops.

Cheap spotted sports shorts.

Plucky Polly played polo.

Tom tried tying Tim's time.

A SHAGGY RACING STORY

Harold, the fastest runner in Alaska, set out to find fame and fortune running marathons. He ran in Boston. He ran in San Francisco. He ran in Los Angeles. Wherever he raced, though, he could not equal the record-breaking time he'd set in Nome.

When the time came for him to run once again in the world-famous Alaskan marathon, Harold was nervous. Could he do it again?

"Don't worry," said his coach. "Just click your heels together three times and say, 'There's no race like Nome.'"

Who's big, round and cold and stands out in the snow shooting arrows?

Frosty the Bowman.

What did the ski instructor say as he heard the weather report?

"Snow news is good news."

Knock-knock.
Who's there?
Ski.
Ski who?
Ski (this key) won't fit the lock.

Knock-Knock.
Who's there?
Randy.
Randy who?
Randy marathon and am I tired!

Knock-Knock.
Who's there?
Tire.
Tire who?
Tire gym shoes—you're about to trip.

Knock-Knock.
Who's there?
Trampoline.
Trampoline who?
Trampoline the grass is not allowed.

12. LIBRARY

What do librarians hang over their babies' cribs?
Bookmobiles.

What has a spine but no bones?
A book.

Why did the Rumanian stop reading for the night?
To give his Bucharest (book a rest).

Why was the library so messy?
Because it was full of litter-ature.

BOOKS & AUTHORS

What do Peter Pan and noon have in common?
Neither have a shadow.

What would you get if you crossed a comedian and an Edgar Allan Poe story?
The wit and the pendulum.

What would you get if you crossed a locomotive with the author of Tom Sawyer?
A choo-choo Twain.

How did the author of Tom Sawyer learn to ride a bicycle?
With Twain-ing wheels.

The Story of Sherwood Forest
by Robin D. Rich

What did they call Tom Sawyer's friend after he lost a lot of weight?
   "Huckleberry thin (Finn)."

What book is about a rodent pioneer?
   "Little Mouse on the Prairie."

Did you read the dachshund's autobiography?
   It's a long story.

What happened when the bloodhound wrote his autobiography?
   It got on the best smeller list.

What books were ordered from Czechoslovakia?
   Czech (check) books.

Which mythological character carried the maps?
   Atlas.

What was the name of the book about a trio of adventurous French cows?
   The Three Moo-sketeers.

13. SEEING THE NURSE

What do you call a yeti with a stomach ache?
  An abdominal snowman.

Why did the water snake need medical attention?
  It felt eel.

What kind of insect has trouble talking?
  The horse (hoarse) fly.

What is the most cowardly disease?
Chicken pox.

What bird transmits the most diseases?
The carrier pigeon.

What shots do rockets get?   *Boosters.*

What kind of pills do astronauts take?
Space capsules.

How did the frog get to the nurse?
He had to be toad (towed).

Knock-Knock.
  Who's there?
Amanda.
  Amanda who?
Amanda a great strain.

Knock-Knock.
  Who's there?
Yule.
  Yule who?
Yule miss me when I'm gone.

Knock-Knock.
  Who's there?
Oslo.
  Oslo who?
Oslo and feeling
bad
today.

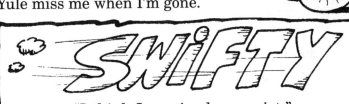

"I think I sprained my wrist,"
Tom said limply.

14. SHOW AND TELL

What do you call a cow with two heads?
A moo-tation.

What do you call a cowardly bird?
Chicken of the tree.

Which is the meanest chicken in the yard?
Attila the hen.

Why do birds lay eggs?
If they dropped them, they'd break.

Where did the shrimp go to sell his watch?
To a prawn shop.

Why wouldn't the oyster give up her pearl?
She was shellfish.

How does an alligator use the telephone?
He croco-dials.

Why couldn't the duck get his medical degree?
He was a quack.

I cannot walk.
I wear no shoe.
I follow you.
What am I?
Your shadow.

Where do spiders get married?
In a webbing chapel.

What is the most disgusting plant?
Yucca.

What are the sneakiest plants?
Creeping vines.

What are the happiest flowers?
Gladiolas.

What Australian animal is a spiritual leader?
Kan-guru.

How does a panda greet a grizzly?
With a bear hug.

Do you know what a grizzly looks like?
Bearly (barely).

What did one porcupine say to the other porcupine?
"Let's get to the point."

What tree has the warmest coat?
The fir.

How do you tell how often a tree has been married?
Count its rings.

What do you call baby fish that drink too fast?
Gulpies (guppies).

What fish was a famous actress?
Marlin Monroe.

Knock-Knock.
    Who's there?
Frieda.
    Frieda who?
Frieda bird from da cage.

What do you call a clumsy lion?
King of the bungle.

What insect tells time?
The clock-roach.

How funny was the snake?
Hiss-sterical.

Knock-Knock.
  Who's there?
Ida Ferris.
  Ida Ferris who?
Ida Ferris one of all.

Knock-Knock.
  Who's there?
Owl.
  Owl who?
Owl I get in the door?

READING LIST!

What Is a Fruit? by Cherry Stone

Not Just a Big Mouse by U.R.A. Rat

How to Deal with Spiders by L.M. Muffet

Reptiles by Sally Mander

How Plants Eat by Oz Moses

Gardening by Rose Busch

What do fishermen's babies wear on their feet?
Boat-tees (booties).

Where do homeless fish live?
On squid (skid) row.

What kind of cable service do preachers watch?
Pray TV.

Knock-Knock.
Who's there?
Tildy.
Tildy who?
Tildy soil so the plants will grow.

TONGUE *Twisters*

...SAY THESE 3 TIMES QUICKLY!..

Fleas feel furry.

Green plants, blue pants, red plants.

Luke likes lemmings.

Seeds and seedlings scared Sally.

Peter planted plums.

15. WHAT DO YOU WANT TO BE?

What do dentists use to glue things together?
Toothpaste.

What do baby highway patrolmen play with?
Road blocks.

Why did the magician quit his job?
He was dis-illusioned.

Why did the boy want to become a chimney sweep?
He felt the job sooted him.

Why did the reporter take a job on a ship?
He wanted to become an anchor man.

Why did the man go to work in the lighthouse?
To bring home the beacon.

What did one cold logger say to the other logger?
"Tim, brrr."

Why does a sasquatch make such a good salesman?
He can easily get his foot in the door.

Why do bakers get so much dough?
They knead (need) it.

Old astronauts never die, they just space out.

Old photographers never die, they just get negative.

Old firemen never die, they just get burned out.

Old radio announcers never die, they just sign off.

Old planters never die, they just go to seed.

Old dentists never die, they just get drilled out of the corps.

Old lions never die, they just bite off more than they can chew.

Old cartoonists never die, they just draw a blank.

Old Egyptians never die, they just sphinx they do.

Old snowmen never die, they just drift away.

Old potato farmers never die, they just don't see eye to eye.

Old movie producers never die, they just fade out.

Old bookkeepers never die, they just lose their balance.

Old clockmakers never die, they just run out of time.

Old tennis players never die, they just leave the racket.

Old boat builders never die, they just go under.

Old telephone operators never die, they just get disconnected.

Old cleaners never die, they just get all washed up.

16. JUST FOR FUN

What kind of trees are used to build kennels?
Dogwood.

What insect sews the best?
The quilting bee.

Why did the girl want to become a seamstress?
To mend her ways.

How well did the girl make her dress?
Sew-sew.

How do you paint an ocean?
With water colors.

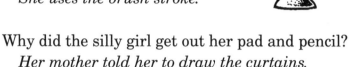

How does a painter swim?
She uses the brush stroke.

Why did the silly girl get out her pad and pencil?
Her mother told her to draw the curtains.

What do cats wear when they go out?
Purr-fume.

Knock-Knock.
  Who's there?
Mold.
  Mold who?
Mold (I'm old) enough to stay up late.

Knock-Knock.
  Who's there?
Eskimo.
  Eskimo who?
Eskimo questions I'll
tell you mo' lies.

Knock-Knock.
  Who's there?
Comma.
  Comma who?
Comma home with me.

Knock-Knock.
  Who's there?
Crater.
  Crater who?
Crater up and
ship her out.

Knock-Knock.
  Who's there?
Dopey.
  Dopey who?
Dopey so stubborn
and open the door.

Knock-Knock.
  Who's there?
Raisin.
  Raisin who?
Raisin Cane.

Knock-Knock.
  Who's there?
Hula.
  Hula who?
Hula-la it's hot today.

Knock-Knock.
  Who's there?
Tennis.
  Tennis who?
Tennis half of twenty.

Knock-Knock.
  Who's there?
Wendy Poole.
  Wendy Poole who?
Wendy Poole gets warmer,
we'll go swimming.

Knock-Knock.
  Who's there?
Museum.
  Museum who?
Museum (you've seen)
one, Museum all.

Knock-Knock.
  Who's there?
Saturn.
  Saturn who?
Little Miss Muffet
Saturn a tuffet...

Why didn't the teacher allow the pig to be in the play?

He was too much of a ham.

Why did the thief want to become a great actor?

So he could steal the show.

What did the motor say to the battery?

"You started it."

Why didn't the deer take anyone to the dance?

He wanted to go stag.

Why wouldn't the owl cross the road?
He didn't give a hoot.

How did the carpenter break his tooth?
Biting his nails.

GOTCHA

YOU: What's your name?
FRIEND: *(tells you).*
YOU: How do you spell it?
FRIEND: *(spells it).*
YOU: Wrong. You spell "it" I-T.

READING LIST!

Cabinet Finishing by Sandy Wood

Carpentry by Sawyer Bord

Breaking Up by Hugo Way

Driftwood by Sandy Beach

Wild Animals by Bob Katz

Dishonest Animals by Cheetah Samoa

Mind Over Matter by Ben D. Spoon

Answering Machines by Colin Bach

Why did the man in armor come down the chimney on December 24th?

It was the knight before Christmas.

What did one Christmas tree say to the other?

"I pine for you."

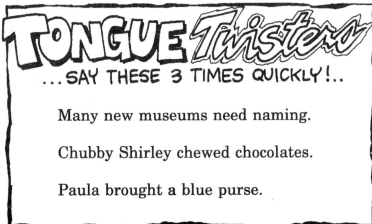

Many new museums need naming.

Chubby Shirley chewed chocolates.

Paula brought a blue purse.

Knock-Knock.
  Who's there?
Cindy.
  Cindy who?
Cindy butler to
open the door.

Knock-Knock.
  Who's there?
Igloo.
  Igloo who?
Igloo the wood together.

"Get that mouse out of here,"
Tom squeaked.

"Let me tell you about male bees,"
Tom droned on.

"That's a silly nickname for Charles,"
Tom chuck-led.

"I think someone put a microphone in my desk,"
Tom was bugged.

"I like California," Tom stated.

17. PRINCIPAL'S OFFICE

WE BOTH KNOW WHAT YOU DID WAS WRONG, BUT LET'S NOT *HARP* ON THAT!...

PRINCIPAL

Why was the little harp sent to the principal's office?
It was a lyre (liar).

Why did the firefly do so well in school?
He was one of the brightest students.

Where do they put rowdy apes?
Behind monkey bars.

What vegetables get in the most trouble?
Cucumbers. They're always in a pickle.

Which teachers are most difficult?

English teachers, because they hand down stiff sentences.

Knock-Knock.
   Who's there?
Arena.
   Arena who?
You arena lot of trouble.

Knock-Knock.
   Who's there?
Tom Sawyer.
   Tom Sawyer who?
Tom Sawyer answers.

Knock-Knock.
   Who's there?
Lionel.
   Lionel who?
Lionel get you nowhere.

Knock-Knock.
   Who's there?
Yacht.
   Yacht who?
Yacht to tell the truth.

Knock-Knock.
   Who's there?
Decimal.
   Decimal who?
Decimal (dismal) marks you've been getting.

18. AFTER SCHOOL

How did the chicken get along with the other animals?
It was always in a fowl (foul) mood.

What kind of pets do mermaids have?
Catfish and dogfish.

What do you call riding your bike twice in one day?
Re-cycling.

Knock-Knock.
 Who's there?
Candy.
 Candy who?
Candy kids come out and play?

Knock-Knock.
 Who's there?
Dune.
 Dune who?
Dune nothing this afternoon.

Knock-Knock.
 Who's there?
Meteor.
 Meteor who?
Want to Meteor new dog.

Knock-Knock.
 Who's there?
Randolph.
 Randolph who?
You Randolph with my lunch.

Knock-Knock.
 Who's there?
Celia.
 Celia who?
Celia later!

Index

95